$$\frac{6}{12}$$

six twelfths

MW00895561

$$\frac{4}{12}$$

four twelfths

$$\frac{3}{12}$$

three twelfths

$$\frac{1}{12}$$

one twelfth

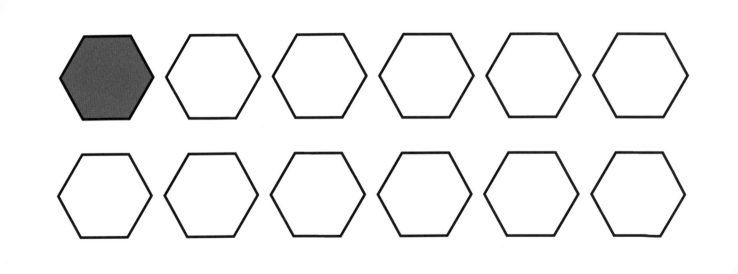

$$\frac{6}{10}$$

six tenths

$$\frac{5}{10}$$

five tenths

$$\frac{4}{10}$$

four tenths

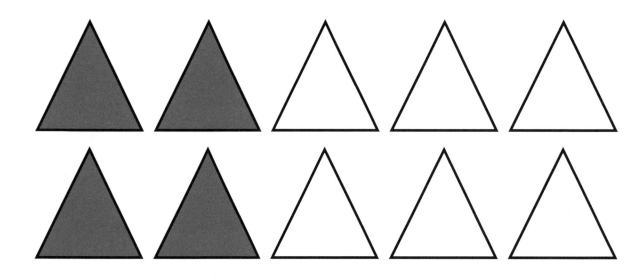

$$\frac{3}{10}$$

three tenths

$$\frac{6}{8}$$

six eighths

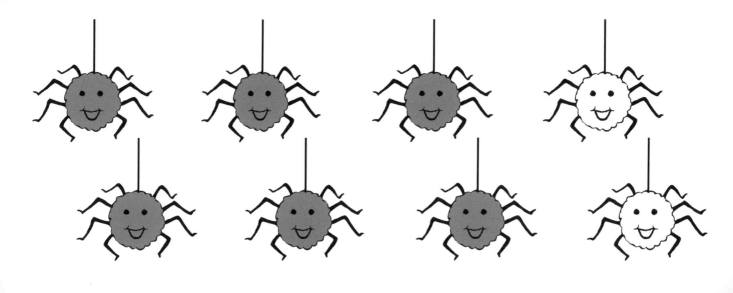

$$\frac{5}{8}$$

five eighths

$$\frac{4}{8}$$

four eighths

$$\frac{2}{8}$$

two eighths

$$\frac{1}{8}$$

one eighth

$$\frac{5}{6}$$

five sixths

$$\frac{4}{6}$$

four sixths

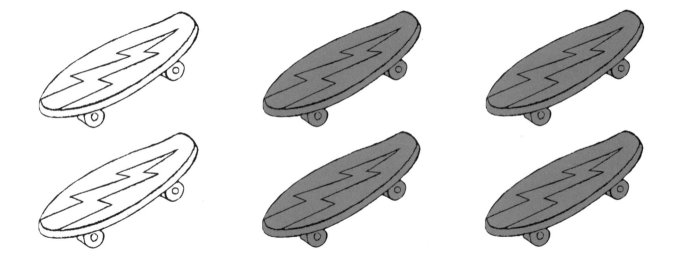

$$\frac{3}{6}$$

three sixths

$$\frac{2}{6}$$

two sixths

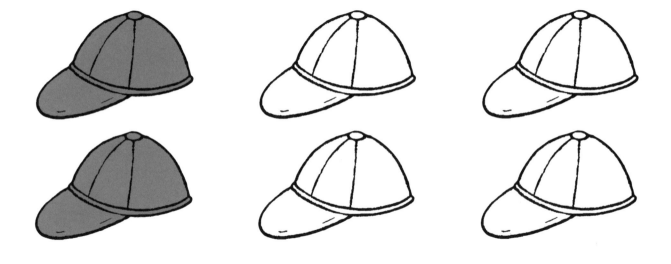

$$\frac{1}{6}$$

one sixth

$$\frac{4}{5}$$

four fifths

$$\frac{3}{5}$$

three fifths

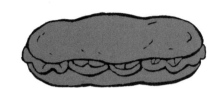 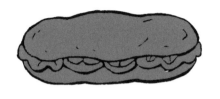 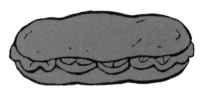

$$\frac{2}{5}$$

two fifths

$$\frac{1}{5}$$

one fifth

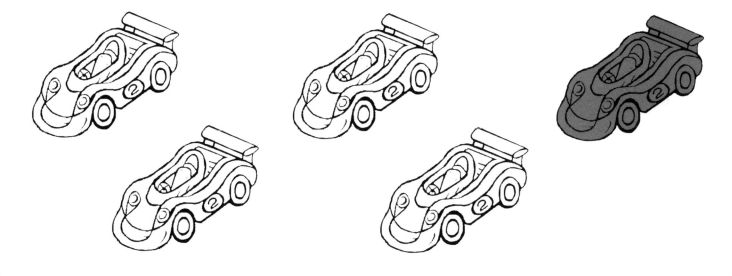

$$\frac{3}{4}$$

three fourths

$$\frac{2}{4}$$

two fourths

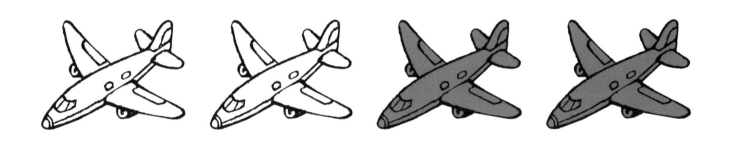

one fourth

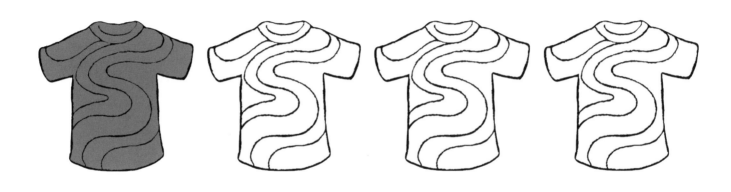

$$\frac{2}{3}$$

two thirds

$$\frac{1}{3}$$

one third

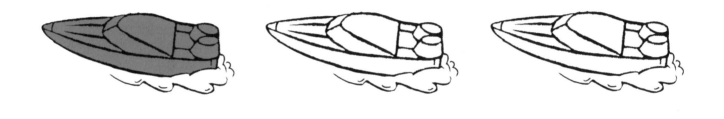

$$\frac{1}{2}$$

one half

$$\frac{12}{12}$$

twelve twelfths

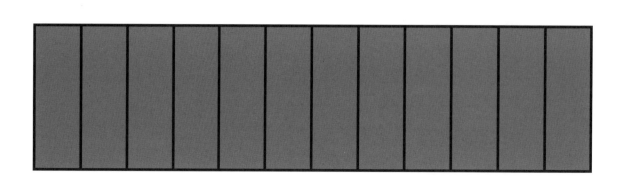

$$\frac{11}{12}$$

eleven twelfths

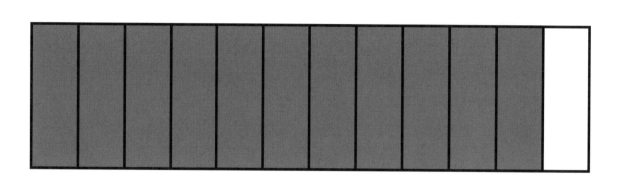

$$\frac{10}{12}$$

ten twelfths

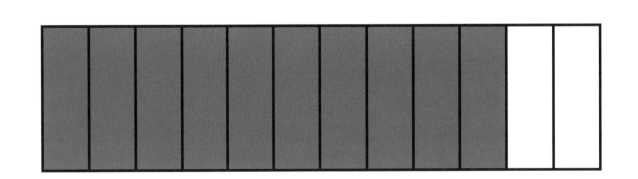

$$\frac{9}{12}$$

nine twelfths

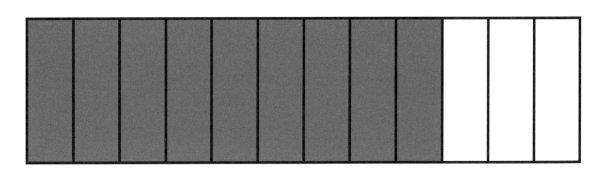

$$\frac{8}{12}$$

eight twelfths

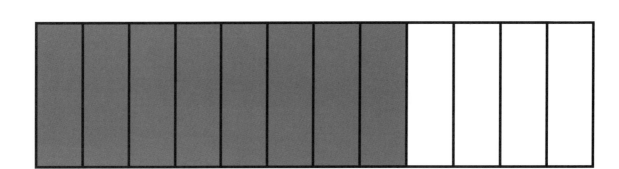

$$\frac{7}{12}$$

seven twelfths

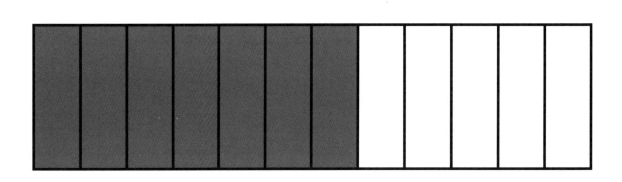

$$\frac{6}{12}$$

six twelfths

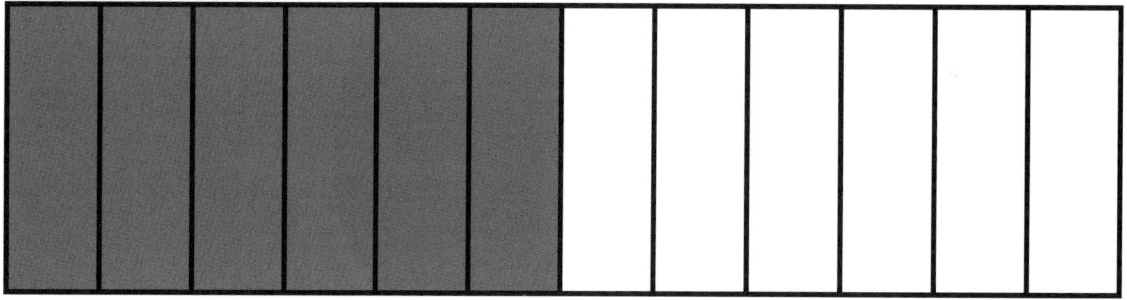

$$\frac{5}{12}$$

five twelfths

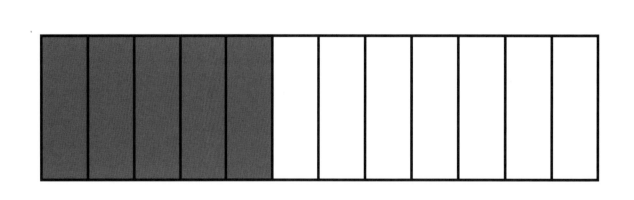

$$\frac{4}{12}$$

four twelfths

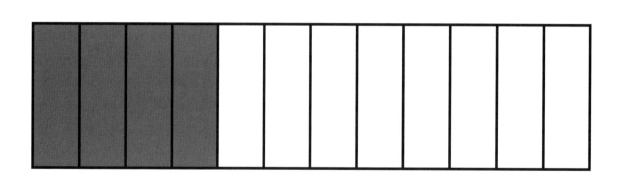

$$\frac{3}{12}$$

three twelfths

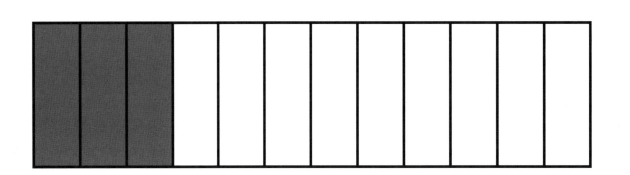

$$\frac{2}{12}$$

two twelfths

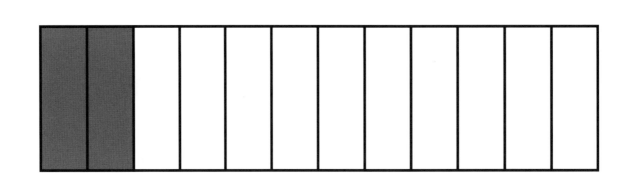

$$\frac{1}{12}$$

one twelfth

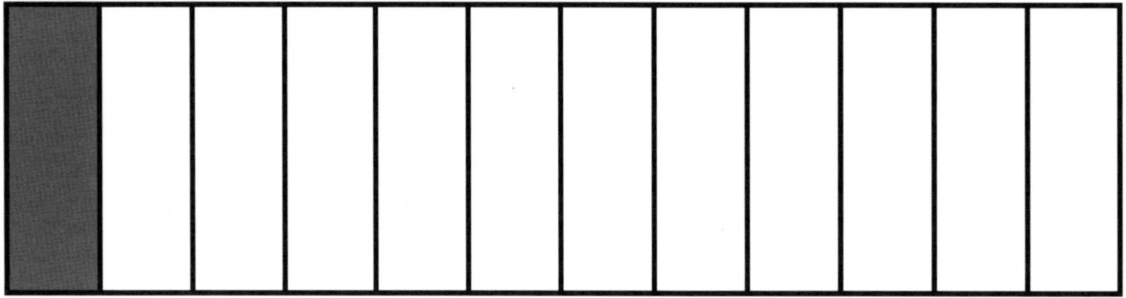

$$\frac{10}{10}$$

ten tenths

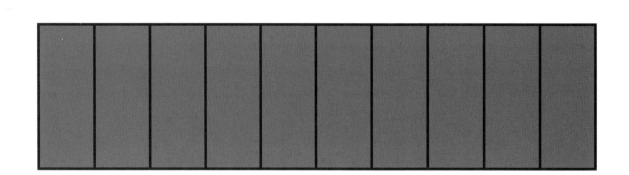

$$\frac{9}{10}$$

nine tenths

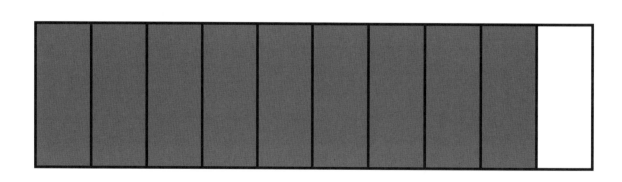

$$\frac{8}{10}$$

eight tenths

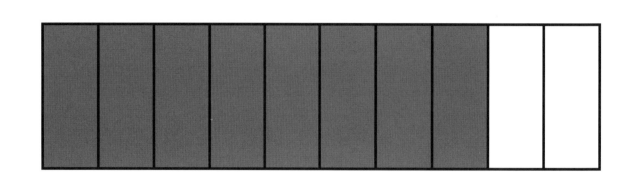

$$\frac{7}{10}$$

seven tenths

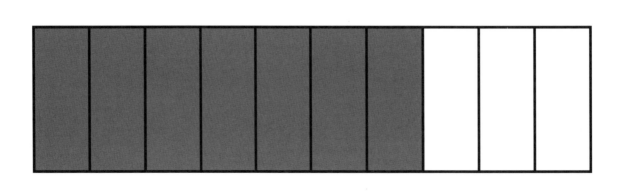

$$\frac{6}{10}$$

six tenths

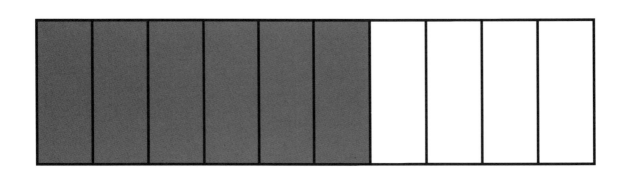

$$\frac{5}{10}$$

five tenths

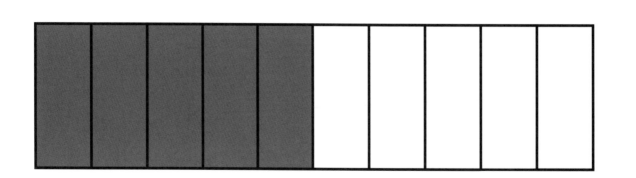

$$\frac{4}{10}$$

four tenths

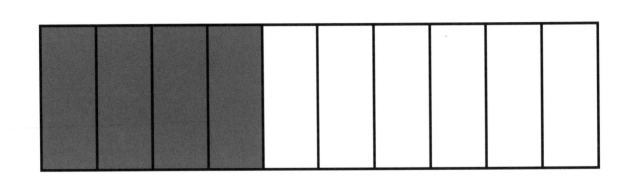

$$\frac{3}{10}$$

three tenths

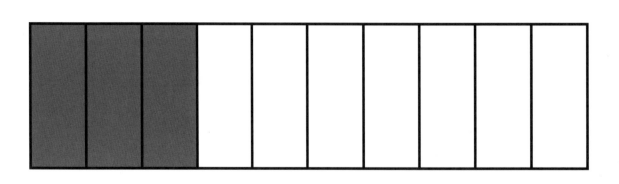

$$\frac{2}{10}$$

two tenths

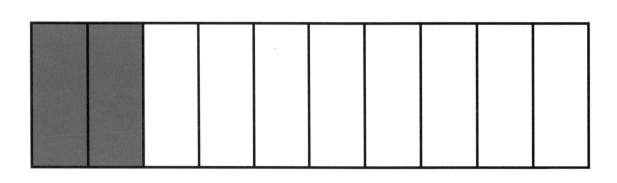

$$\frac{1}{10}$$

one tenth

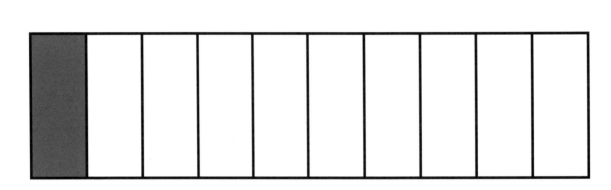

$$\frac{8}{8}$$

eight eighths

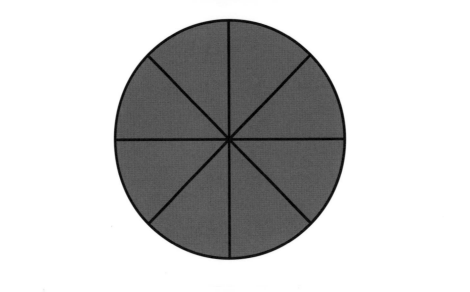

$$\frac{7}{8}$$

seven eighths

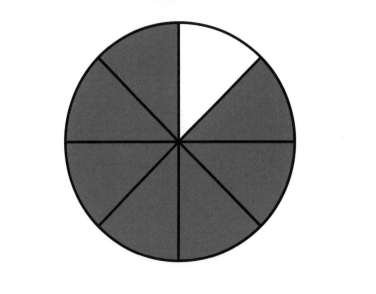

$$\frac{6}{8}$$

six eighths

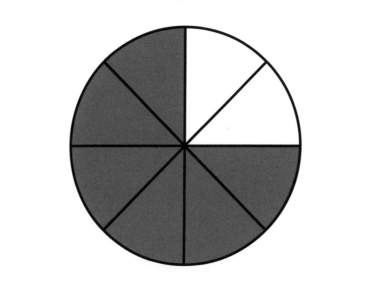

$$\frac{5}{8}$$

five eighths

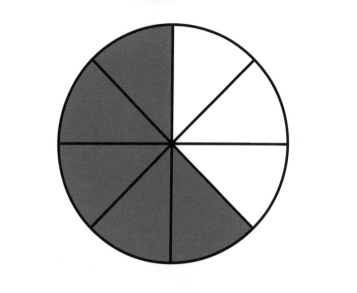

$$\frac{4}{8}$$

four eighths

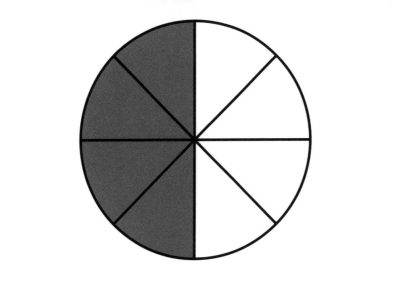

$\dfrac{3}{8}$ three eighths

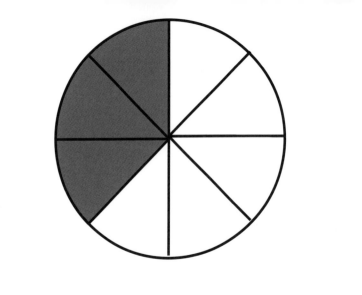

$$\frac{2}{8}$$

two eighths

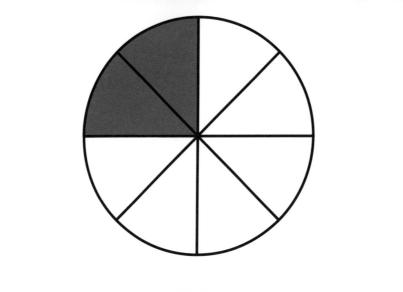

$$\frac{1}{8}$$

one eighth

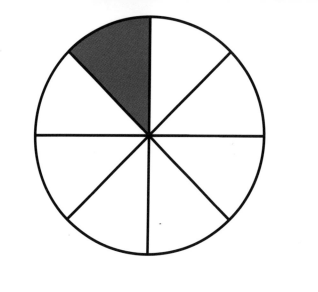

$$\frac{6}{6}$$

six sixths

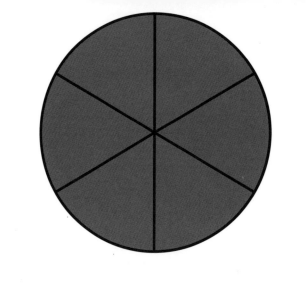

$$\frac{5}{6}$$

five sixths

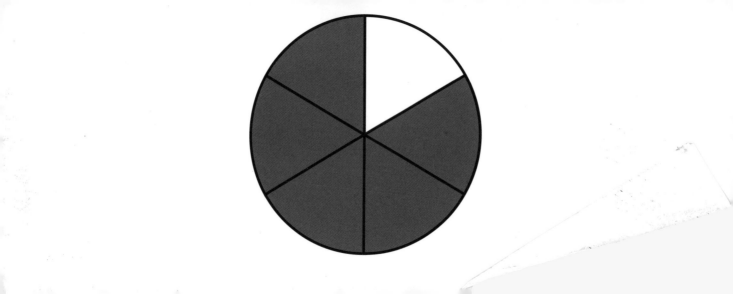

$$\frac{4}{6}$$

four sixths

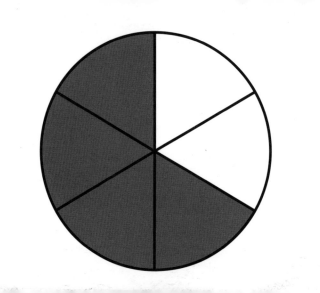

$$\frac{3}{6}$$

three sixths

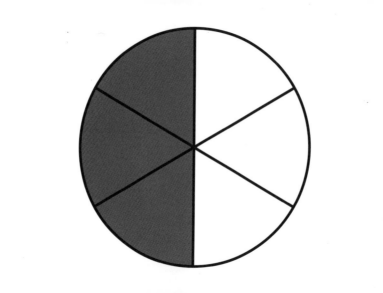

$$\frac{2}{6}$$

two sixths

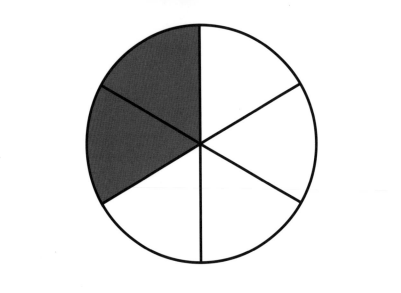

$$\frac{1}{6}$$

one sixth

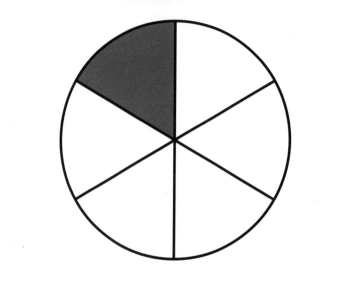

$$\frac{5}{5}$$

five fifths

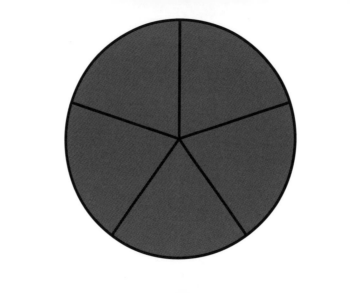

$$\frac{4}{5}$$

four fifths

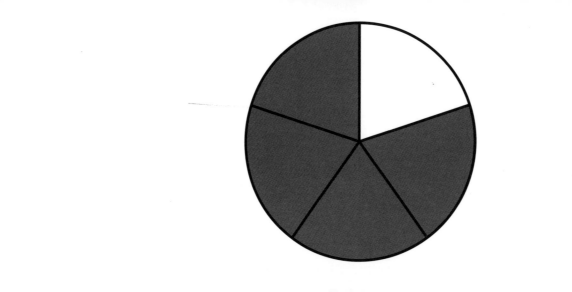

$$\frac{3}{5}$$

three fifths

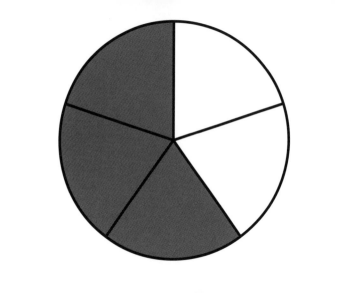

$$\frac{2}{5}$$

two fifths

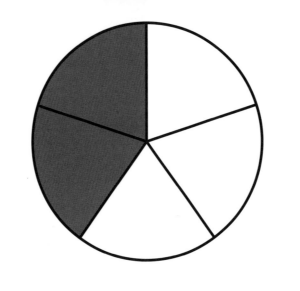

$$\frac{1}{5}$$

one fifth

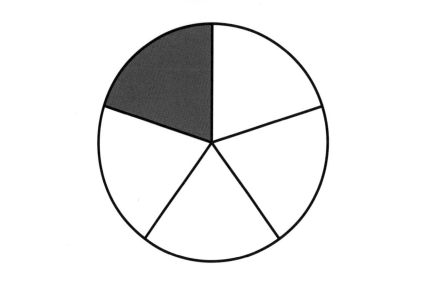

$$\frac{4}{4}$$

four fourths

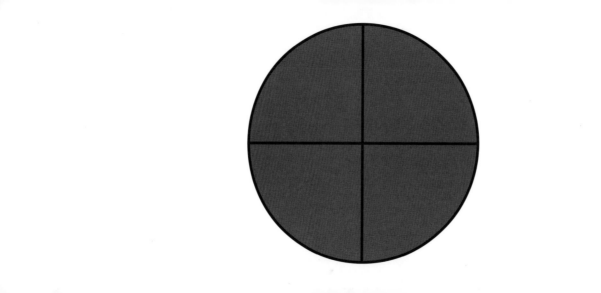

$$\frac{3}{4}$$

three fourths

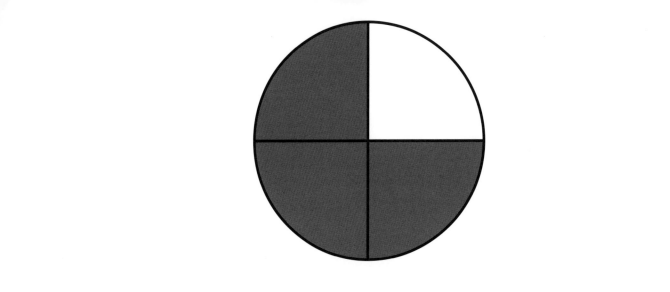

$$\frac{2}{4}$$

two fourths

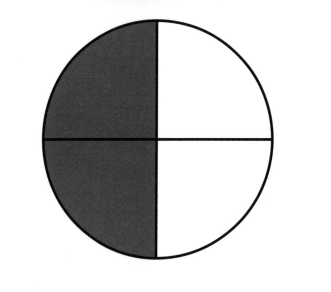

$$\frac{1}{4}$$

one fourth

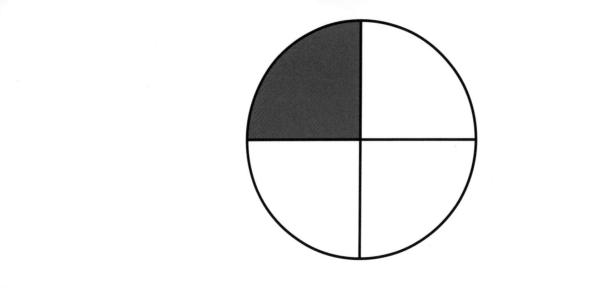

$$\frac{3}{3}$$ **three thirds**

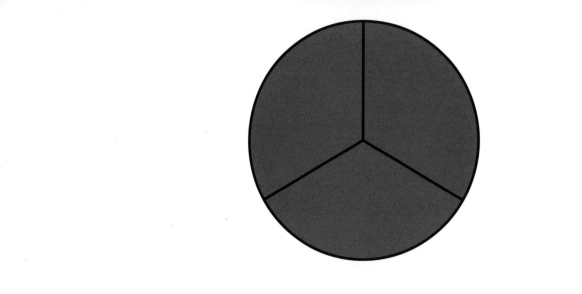

$$\frac{2}{3}$$

two thirds

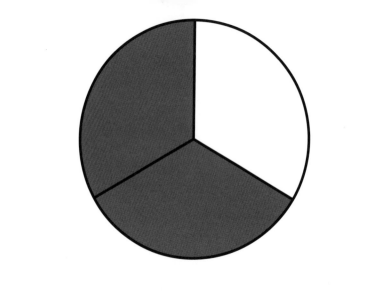

$$\frac{1}{3}$$

one third

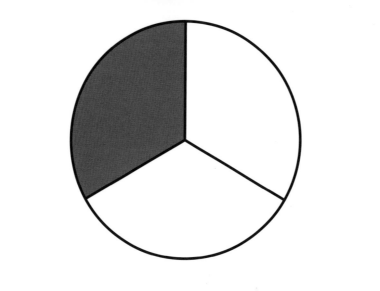

$$\frac{2}{2}$$

two halves

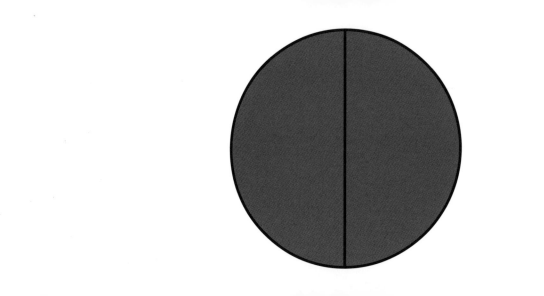

$$\frac{1}{2}$$

one half

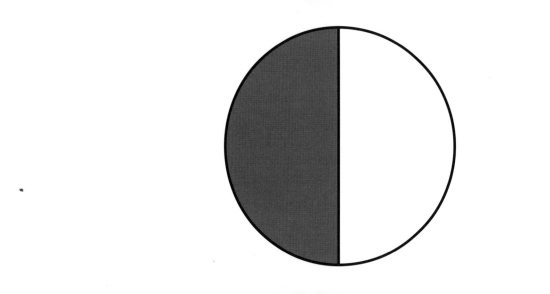

Some Equivalent Fractions

$\frac{1}{2} = \frac{2}{4}, \frac{3}{6}, \frac{4}{8}, \frac{5}{10}, \frac{6}{12}$			
$\frac{1}{3} = \frac{2}{6}, \frac{4}{12}$ $\quad$ $\frac{2}{3} = \frac{4}{6}, \frac{8}{12}$			
$\frac{1}{4} = \frac{2}{8}, \frac{3}{12}$ $\quad$ $\frac{3}{4} = \frac{6}{8}, \frac{9}{12}$			
$\frac{1}{5} = \frac{2}{10}$	$\frac{2}{5} = \frac{4}{10}$	$\frac{3}{5} = \frac{6}{10}$	$\frac{4}{5} = \frac{8}{10}$
$\frac{1}{6} = \frac{2}{12}$	$\frac{2}{6} = \frac{4}{12}$	$\frac{4}{6} = \frac{8}{12}$	$\frac{5}{6} = \frac{10}{12}$

Make It a Game Try finding fractions that are greater than or less than a fraction that someone chooses. Make a list of the equivalent fractions.

Why Do We Need Fractions Anyway? Think about it. When do you use fractions? When do you see other people using fractions? Ask people why they use fractions. Make a list of the ways people use fractions.

Helpful Hints for Learning Fractions

Flip and Check Name the fraction that describes the shaded pieces of the pictorial model on one side, then flip the page to check your answer.

$\frac{2}{3}$ two thirds	$\frac{4}{5}$ four fifths

Show the Fractions Duplicate the fraction models and cut them out. Use the pieces to show the fractions.

Frank Schaffer Publications®

Published by Ideal School Supply
An imprint of Frank Schaffer Publications
Copyright © 2000 School Specialty Publishing

All Rights Reserved • Printed in China

No part of this publication may be reproduced, stored in a retrieval system, or transmitted, in any form or by any means, electronic, mechanical, photocopying, recording, or otherwise, without the pr͟i͟o͟r͟ ͟w͟r͟i͟t͟t͟e͟n͟ ͟p͟e͟r͟m͟i͟s͟s͟i͟o͟n͟ of the publisher.

Send all inquiries to:
Frank Schaffer Publications
3195 Wilson Drive NW
Grand Rapids, Michigan 49534

Flip-Flash™ Math: Fractions

6 7 8 9 10 11 12 WKT 10 09 08 07

ISBN 1-56451-350-5

9 781564 513502

MW00895561